The Mighty Pollinators

poems by

Helen Frost

photographs by

Rick Lieder

CANDLEWICK PRESS

Almost Invisible

When you're outside on a
    summer day,
have you sneezed and
    wondered why?
Have you seen fine powder
at the heart of a flower
as bumblebees buzz by?

It's pollen in the air,
pollen in the flowers,
pollen helping plants make seeds.
Almost invisible, pollen waits
for the only thing it needs—
a ride on the wind
or on wing,
fur,
or feather.

Here come the pollinators,
small and mighty,
holding the world together.

Bees

Bumblebees
on apple blossoms,
honey bees
on clover.
We're the bees
that carry pollen
to our hive.

Solitary sweat bees,
no-bigger-than-an-ant bees.

We're on the front lines,
keeping fruit and flowers
    alive.

Ants

We climb onto a flower
and turn ourselves around.
Let's nod our heads in greeting
and shake some pollen down!

Wasps

Cover up
    your jelly sandwich.
Watch us
    when we fly away.
We'll show you
    where to find
        sweet nectar
on this bright
    sunny day.

Flies

Not every flower
    is colorful, bright.
Not every bloom
    smells sweet.

Some of us also love
brown and white,
and the smell of
rotten meat.

Butterflies

We drink from summer flowers.
Their nectar fuels our flight.
We carry pollen on our wings
as we lift into the light.

Clover to cabbage to sunflower—
see us flutter by?
Zinnia. Hollyhock.
Dawn to dusk
is the realm of the butterfly.

Moths

What happens after the sun goes down
and butterflies rest in the trees?
This is our time.
We're the beautiful moths,
riding the evening breeze.

Our antennae,
like feather dusters,
sweep pollen from the flowers.
We carry it over the sleeping world—
dusk to dawn is ours.

Bats

After resting on night-blooming flowers,
we have pollen in our fur
when we rise into the star-filled sky.
Through woods
and over moonlit meadows,
we catch moths and mosquitoes as we fly.

Fireflies

If you've only seen us
flashing in a meadow
on a dark July or August night

you might not notice
how we rest on flower petals
when summer days are hot
    and bright.

The flowers dust
our folded wings and black
    antennae
with pollen, gold or white,

trusting us
to spread their treasure
each time we take flight.

Wind

You may not see me,
but you know I'm here
when I brush past your skin.
Strong and fierce
or soft and gentle,
I'm pollen's good friend—
I'm the wind.

What Is Pollen?

Pollen is a fine powder made of tiny grains, usually yellow, orange, or white. Each grain by itself is almost too small to see, but if you look closely at a flower, you may see pollen as a fine dust or in small clumps. Sometimes you can also see it on the ground beneath flowers or on the surface of nearby water. If you shake a flower over dark paper, pollen may land on the paper, where it will be easier to see.

Pollen is important because it helps plants make seeds, which are needed in order to make new plants. Much of the food we eat depends on pollen and pollination.

What Is Pollination?

Pollen forms on one part of a flower, the anther, and must be moved to another part, the stigma, and from there to the ovary, where seeds are formed. It may be moved from the anther to the stigma of the same flower or from the anther of one flower to the stigma of a different flower of the same species.

This movement of pollen is pollination.

Pollinators help with the important job of pollination. For example, when a bee stops at one flower to get pollen or nectar, some pollen brushes off the anther of that flower onto the bee. Then, when the bee flies to another flower, carrying the pollen on its body, some of it falls onto the second flower's stigma. From there, it will move to the ovary.

Pollen is moved by different pollinators in many ways. In addition to the pollinators you've seen in this book, hummingbirds, small animals, mosquitoes, spiders, and even people can all contribute to pollination.

Observing Pollinators

You can learn more about pollinators by observing them closely. Go outdoors and find a flower. If you stand back a few feet and watch it, you may see bees, flies, butterflies, and other pollinators visiting the flower. If they leave that flower and go to another one, they are probably carrying pollen with them and pollinating that flower. Keep watching to see how many different pollinators you can see.

Don't be afraid of any pollinators that may sting, but don't disturb them, either. Watch them from a safe distance.

Helping Pollinators

We can help the pollinators by protecting wildflowers and by planting special pollinator gardens. Native flowers and pollinators are especially important. Ask a librarian or other adult to help you find out which ones are native to your area.

Different kinds of flowers attract different kinds of pollinators, so let a variety of wildflowers grow and spread. Flowers such as dandelions and clover, sometimes thought of as weeds, are important sources of pollen and nectar, especially in early spring. Milkweed and Queen Anne's lace are some of the many plants that are essential food for the caterpillars that will soon become butterflies and moths.

If you plant a garden for flowers or food, don't use anything in your garden that is made to kill plants or insects.

As you enjoy your garden, you will become a Mighty Pollinator Protector!

For Annika Marie and Kira Grace
HF

For all the small and mighty friends who make our life on earth possible, and for Kathe
RL

Special thanks to Dr. Timothy Gibb, entomologist; Sarah Ketchersid, editor; and Hayley Parker and Martha Kennedy, designers.

The Pollinators in This Book

Rick Lieder photographed all the pollinators featured in this book near his home in southeastern Michigan.

Front jacket: cabbage white butterfly. Front jacket flap: grass-carrying wasp. Front endpaper: sweat bee. Title page: (main image) sweat bee, (insets, left to right) carpenter ant, fiery skipper butterfly, sweat bee. "Bees": (first spread, main image) bumblebee, (top inset) mason bee, (bottom insets, left to right) honey bee, honey bee, bumblebee; (second spread) sweat bee. "Ants": (main image and all insets except winged ant) odorous house ant, (winged ant) carpenter ant. "Wasps": mason wasp. "Flies": (left inset) syrphid fly, (middle inset) margined calligrapher hoverfly, (top right inset) fruit fly, (bottom right inset) margined calligrapher hoverfly, (main image) housefly. "Butterflies": (main image) cabbage white butterfly, (top insets, left to right) silver-spotted skipper butterfly, pearl crescent butterfly, cabbage white butterfly, (bottom inset) cabbage white butterfly. "Moths": ailanthus webworm moth. "Bats": big brown bat. "Fireflies": (all images) common eastern firefly. "Wind": honey bee. Information pages: (left to right) orchard orb-weaver spider, northern house mosquito. Back endpaper: carpenter bee. Back jacket flap: silver-spotted skipper butterfly. Back jacket: bumblebee.